MATH IN ACTION

SUBTRACTION

Joan Felder

FEARON / JANUS / QUERCUS
Belmont, California

FEARON
JANUS
QUERCUS

Publishers for
Special Needs

Math in Action Series

Addition
Subtraction
Multiplication
Division
Mixed Numbers
Simple Fractions
Decimals and Percents
Measuring
Mathtactics

Word Problems
  Math Language
  Understanding Word Problems
  Using a Calculator
  Estimation
  Solving Word Problems
  Word Problems Teacher's Guide & Resource

Illustrator: Margaret Sanfilippo
Cover Design: Joe C. Shines

Consultant: Michael A. Contino
          Director, Entry Level Math Program
          California State University, Hayward

Math in Action: Subtraction
ISBN 0-8224-4493-3

Printed in the United States of America
1. 9 8 7 6 5 4 3

Contents

Introduction

Let's say you work in an office. Each morning you must spend 60 minutes making telephone calls to customers that are on a list.

This morning, after you make several calls, your boss asks how many customers are left on the list. Your boss also wants to know how many more minutes you will spend on this job. When your time is up, you must write down how many more people you called today than yesterday.

Those are examples of math problems that can happen on a job. To solve them, you must *subtract* an amount from another amount. Those are also examples of times when you must give *correct* answers.

You will have to subtract many times in real life, not just on your job. Will you subtract correctly? Suppose someone such as a sales person subtracts an amount for you. Will you be able to tell whether that person has made a mistake?

This book can help you subtract correctly *all the time.* It will also help you know when other people have made mistakes. You will learn about whole numbers and what you must do to subtract correctly. You will also learn how to check your answers and how to estimate.

When you are finished with this book, you will have skills that can help you any time you need to subtract—whether you are working with numbers on a job, making a budget for yourself, or having fun with friends.

Before You Start

Subtracting Whole Numbers

Think about the last time you subtracted in real life. You probably used whole numbers—numbers that stand for whole amounts. Whole numbers are the kind of numbers people use the most: you see them on signs and schedules. You read them in magazines, newspapers, and books. You write them on checks and order forms. And you use them to figure with.

For the next several weeks, you will work on improving your ability to subtract whole numbers. You will work better if you have an understanding of our *number system*: how numbers are made, what they are made from, and how they show amounts.

This unit reviews some important ideas about our number system. You may have already studied about our number system, but don't skip over this review. It will help you understand why you must do certain things to subtract correctly.

As you work through this book, you will use certain math words over and over. The words are listed at the right. Make sure you know what the words mean. You'll find their meanings in a *glossary* at the end of this book.

A word about the glossary: the words in the glossary are used to describe all four basic math operations. So, you'll find words there that describe addition, subtraction, multiplication, and division.

Math Words: Subtraction

If you know the meaning of a math word, write a sentence using the word correctly. If you are not sure of a word, look it up in the glossary at the end of this book and write its meaning.

answer bar	opposite
column	place
difference	place value
digit	regroup
estimate	round
exact numbers	set up
line up	symbol

About Our Number System

People who lived in very ancient times did not have numbers to figure with. They probably counted by using their fingers. For example, they might have held up nine fingers to show how many deer they hunted. They might have held up five fingers to show how many of the deer they killed.

In time, people invented words and **symbols** to stand for *amounts*. Those amounts are what we call *numbers*. People also invented ways to put numbers in order and to figure with them. The way people put numbers in order is called a *number system*.

When you count, or subtract, or use any of the other basic math operations, you are using a number system that is based on inventions that were developed long ago. Think of the way you write whole numbers. Did you know that you use just *ten* symbols to write any whole number? Around 200 B.C., the Hindus of India invented a way to use just ten symbols to stand for any amount. Their ideas were spread by Arab traders to Europe, where they developed into the number system you use today.

Exercise

Choose one of these to do. (Choose a topic or activity you have never done before.)

1. Another word for *number* is *numeral*. Find out about one of these numeral systems. Make a report about it.

Egyptian numeral system   Babylonian numeral system
Greek numeral system   Hindu-Arabic numeral system
Roman numeral system

2. Make up your own number system. First decide how many basic symbols your system will have. Then make up those symbols. Next, decide how to use those symbols to show large amounts.

Digits in Places

You use whole numbers every day to count and describe whole amounts. For example, you might count 5 minutes left in class. You might pay $12 for a ticket. You might have 150 papers to deliver. You might read about the speed of light, which is 186,282 miles a second.

Every number from smallest to largest is made up of symbols called **digits**. There are just 10 digits in our number system:

0, 1, 2, 3, 4, 5, 6, 7, 8, 9

Each digit in a number fills a certain **place**. For example, the number 246 has three digits. They fill three places:

2   4   6

- first place
- second place
- third place

The first place is filled by the digit 6. The second place is filled by the digit 4. The third place is filled by the digit 2.

Look at the chart at the right. It shows a nine-digit number and the name of each place the number fills. The name of the first place is the *ones place*. The name of the second place is the *tens place*. What is the name of the third place?

Find the digit 7 in the number on the chart. What is the name of that place?

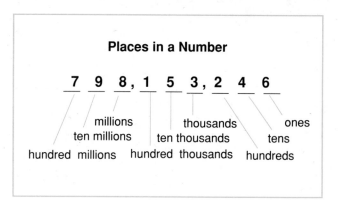

Places in a Number

7   9   8 , 1   5   3 , 2   4   6

millions   thousands   ones
ten millions   ten thousands   tens
hundred millions   hundred thousands   hundreds

Exercise

1. Write the following:
   a. the digits of our number system.
   b. a two-digit number.
   c. a three-digit number.

2. Look at the number on the chart above. Write the digit that fills:
   a. the ten thousands place.
   b. the ten millions place.

Groups of Places

Look at the way this large number is written:

798,153, 246

The number is made up of nine digit-filled places and two *commas*. The commas separate the places into *groups of places*. Each group has three places—a first place, a second place, and a third place.

The chart on the right shows the names of the groups. Notice this: each group is named after its first place. So, 246 fills the *ones group*. 153 fills the *thousands group*. What group does 798 fill?

Each comma separates two groups of places. For example, a comma separates the ones group from the thousands group. Another comma separates the thousands group from the millions group.

Now look at the list of numbers. It shows when a comma is written in a number. Look at the numbers that have commas in them. Notice this: at least one digit must fill the group *before* a comma. How many digits must fill the group *behind* the comma?

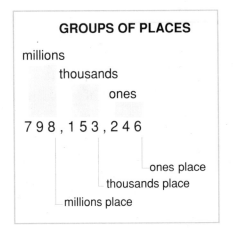

GROUPS OF PLACES

Numbers	
6	
4 6	
2 4 6	
3, 2 4 6	
5 3, 2 4 6	
1 5 3, 2 4 6	
8, 1 5 3, 2 4 6	
9 8, 1 5 3, 2 4 6	
7 9 8, 1 5 3, 2 4 6	

Exercise

1. Copy each number. Draw a line under the underlined group. Then write the name of that group.

   a. 280
   b. 460,280,765
   c. 7,084
   d. 585,772,351
   e. 8,065,136

2. Copy each number. Then write commas where they belong. (Hint: Count from the right.)

   a. 92531
   b. 6498
   c. 13287
   d. 702341807
   e. 1052749

Different Places Mean Different Values

You know that whole numbers are made up of digits in places. Each place has a certain **place value**. That means each place stands for a different *kind of amount*. For example, the first place has a value of *ones*, the second place has a value of *tens*, the third place has a value of *hundreds*.

When a digit fills a place, it stands for a certain amount. That amount depends on the value of the place. Look at the chart. It shows how the *same* digit stands for *different* amounts when it fills *different* places. The squares above each place show the amount that the digit stands for in that place:

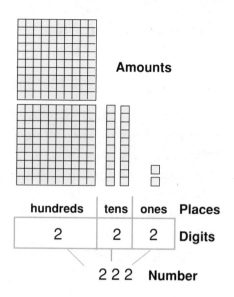

Amounts

hundreds	tens	ones	Places
2	2	2	Digits

2 2 2   Number

2 in the ones place stands for 2 ones, or 2 single things.

2 in the tens place stands for 2 tens, or 2 groups of ten things.

2 in the hundreds place stands for 2 hundreds, or 2 groups of a hundred things.

What would a 2 in the thousands place stand for? 2 in the ten thousands place?

Now look at the squares on the chart. Notice this: in each ten, there are 10 ones. In each hundred, there are 10 tens. Think of this: how many hundreds are in a thousand? How many thousands in ten thousand?

Exercise

1. Write the correct words to complete each sentence. (One is done.)
   a. A 6 in the tens place stands for 6 *tens*, *or 6 groups of ten things.*
   b. A 9 in the ten thousands place stands for 9 __?__ .
   c. A 2 in the millions place stands for 2 __?__ .
   d. A 0 (zero) in the ones place stands for 0 __?__ .

2. Complete each sentence. (One is done.)
   a. 10 ones = 1 *ten*
   b. 10 tens = 1 __?__
   c. 10 hundreds = 1 __?__
   d. 10 thousands = 1 __?__

Working with Numbers in Parts

Suppose you are a bank teller. You need to count out money. What is an easy way to count out this amount?

$345

You can count the amount in parts. You know the 3 stands for *3 hundreds*. The 4 stands for *4 tens*. And the 5 stands for *5 ones*. So, you count out 3 hundred-dollar bills, 4 ten-dollar bills, and 5 one-dollar bills.

When you count and figure amounts, you do the same thing: you work with numbers in parts. Each part of a number is *a digit in a certain place.*

For example, find the number 345 on the chart below. Notice that 345 has three digits in three places. So, 345 has three parts:

3 hundreds and **4 tens** and **5 ones**

hundreds   tens   ones

The chart also shows the number 7,682. How many parts does that number have?

millions	hundred thousands	ten thousands	thousands	hundreds	tens	ones	Places
				3	4	5	= 345
			7	6	8	2	= 7,682

The number 7,682 has four parts:

7 thousands and **6 hundreds** and **8 tens** and **2 ones**

Exercise
Show the parts of each number listed below. Use the chart above to help you. (One is done as an example.)

1. 406 = 4 hundreds and 0 tens and 6 ones

2. 15 = ?

3. 3,683 = ?

4. 42,597 = ?

5. 803,246 = ?

Regrouping

When you solve math problems, you will often have to **_regroup_** an amount. To regroup means to think of an amount of one place value (such as *ones*) as an equal amount of another place value (such as *tens*.) For example, a penny is one cent, and a dime is ten cents. You can think of 10 pennies as the same as 1 dime. And you can think of 23 pennies as the same as 2 dimes and 3 pennies. These pictures show how the one cents are regrouped:

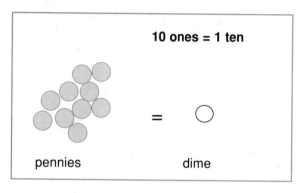

10 ones = 1 ten

pennies   dime

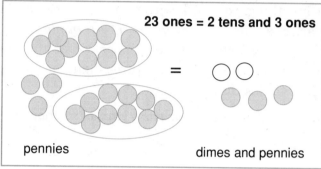

23 ones = 2 tens and 3 ones

pennies   dimes and pennies

Notice this: only amounts of *10 pennies* are regrouped.

Whenever an amount in a place is *more than 9*, it is regrouped. So, 10 ones is regrouped as 1 ten, 10 tens is regrouped as 1 hundred, 10 hundreds is regrouped as 1 thousand, and so on. The chart on the next page lists the ways ones, tens, and hundreds are regrouped.

You can regroup a number according to each of its places. For example:

15 = 15 ones
    or 1 ten and 5 ones

253 = 253 ones
    or 25 tens and 3 ones
    or 2 hundreds and 5 tens and 3 ones

4,638 = 4,638 ones
    or 463 tens and 8 ones
    or 46 hundreds and 3 tens and 8 ones
    or 4 thousands and 6 hundreds and 3 tens and 8 ones

Regrouping Amounts That Are More Than 9

hundreds to thousands	tens to hundreds	ones to tens

	thousands hundreds tens ones		hundreds tens ones		tens ones
10 hundreds = 1 thousand	1,0 0 0	10 tens = 1 hundred	1 0 0	10 ones = 1 ten	1 0
20 hundreds = 2 thousands	2,0 0 0	20 tens = 2 hundreds	2 0 0	20 ones = 2 tens	2 0
30 hundreds = 3 thousands	3,0 0 0	30 tens = 3 hundreds	3 0 0	30 ones = 3 tens	3 0
40 hundreds = 4 thousands	4,0 0 0	40 tens = 4 hundreds	4 0 0	40 ones = 4 tens	4 0
50 hundreds = 5 thousands	5,0 0 0	50 tens = 5 hundreds	5 0 0	50 ones = 5 tens	5 0
60 hundreds = 6 thousands	6,0 0 0	60 tens = 6 hundreds	6 0 0	60 ones = 6 tens	6 0
70 hundreds = 7 thousands	7,0 0 0	70 tens = 7 hundreds	7 0 0	70 ones = 7 tens	7 0
80 hundreds = 8 thousands	8,0 0 0	80 tens = 8 hundreds	8 0 0	80 ones = 8 tens	8 0
90 hundreds = 9 thousands	9,0 0 0	90 tens = 9 hundreds	9 0 0	90 ones = 9 tens	9 0

Exercise

Regroup each number according to its places. Follow the example.

1. 51 = _?_ ones

   or   _?_ tens and _?_ one

2. 35 = _?_ ones

   or   _?_ tens and _?_ ones

3. 514 = _?_ ones

   or   _?_ tens and _?_ ones

   or   _?_ hundreds and _?_ ten and _?_ ones

4. 872 = _?_ ones

   or   _?_ tens and _?_ ones

   or   _?_ hundreds and _?_ tens and _?_ ones

5. 1,346 = _?_ ones

   or   _?_ tens and _?_ ones

   or   _?_ hundreds and _?_ tens and _?_ ones

   or   _?_ thousand and _?_ hundreds and _?_ tens and _?_ ones

6. 3,012 = _?_ ones

   or   _?_ tens and _?_ ones

   or   _?_ hundreds and _?_ ten and _?_ ones

   or   _?_ thousands and _?_ hundreds and _?_ ten and _?_ ones

> **Example:**
> 308 = 308 ones
>   or 30 tens and 8 ones
>   or 3 hundreds and 0 tens and 8 ones

13

Rounding Numbers

To figure problems, you will sometimes **round** the numbers you work with. In other words, you will change them so that they end in zeros. For example, suppose you work 23 hours one week. You might say, "I worked *about 20* hours." Or, suppose you save $114. You might say, "I have *about $100* saved."

When you change 23 to *about* 20 or 114 to *about* 100, you change an **exact number** to a round number. The round number shows an amount that is close to the exact number. But the round number is easier to use.

To see why, look at the examples below. The top number in each example is the exact number. The bottom number is the round number that shows *about* the same amount.

Examples of Rounding

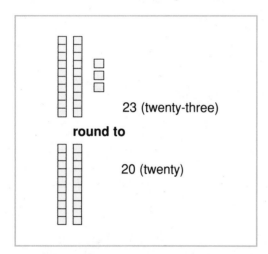

23 (twenty-three)

round to

20 (twenty)

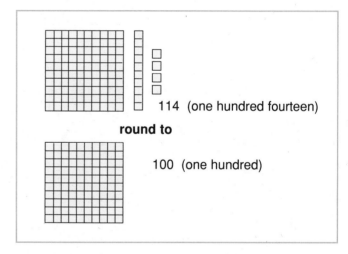

114 (one hundred fourteen)

round to

100 (one hundred)

Notice this: in each example, the round number has only one digit that is not a zero. So, the round number is easier to write. It is also easier to read and easier to keep in your mind. Why is that?

Exercise

Copy the numbers in each problem. Then circle the *round* number.

1. 20   24

2. 389   400

3. 216   200

4. 7,000   6,903

Rounding Down or Up to a Place

When you round an exact number, you round it to a place. You change it to a round ten, round hundred, round thousand, or a larger round number. The chart at the right shows round tens, hundreds, and thousands. Notice this about each round number: after the place farthest left, every place is filled with zero. For example: 9**0**, 9**00**, and 9,**000**.

Round Tens	Round Hundreds	Round Thousands
90	900	9,000
80	800	8,000
70	700	7,000
60	600	6,000
50	500	5,000
40	400	4,000
30	300	3,000
20	200	2,000
10	100	1,000

You round a number *down* or *up* to a place. When you round it down, you change it to the closest *smaller* round number in that place. When you round it up, you change it to the closest *larger* round number in that place. Here's how to round a number down or up:

To round a number down to a place:
1. Do not change the digit in the place.
2. Change all digits right of that place to zeros.

$$64 \approx 60 \qquad 924 \approx 900 \qquad 5{,}248 \approx 5{,}000$$

To round a number up to a place:
1. Change the digit in the place to the next higher digit.
2. Change all digits right of that place to zeros.

$$69 \approx 70 \qquad 954 \approx 1{,}000 \qquad 5{,}848 \approx 6{,}000$$

To show an exact number and its rounded number, use the symbol $\approx$. It stands for *is about equal to*.

Exercise

1. Round each number down or up to the tens place. (Two are done as examples.)

Round down	**Round up**
a. 43 $43 \approx 40$	**d.** 46 $46 \approx 50$
b. 92	**e.** 97
c. 44	**f.** 45

2. Round each number down or up to the hundreds place.

Round down	**Round up**
a. 639	**d.** 856
b. 238	**e.** 289
c. 129	**f.** 199

3. Round each number down or up to the thousands place.

Round down	**Round up**
a. 4,206	**d.** 4,706
b. 6,279	**e.** 5,642
c. 4,034	**f.** 1,930

15

The Nearest Round Number

When you round numbers to help you solve problems, you must round them up or down to the *nearest* ten, hundred, thousand, and so on. That's because a round number should be as close as possible to the actual number it stands for. Here is how to round a number to the nearest place:

Rounding Down or Up to the Nearest Place:

Examples: 346   356

1. Look at the digit in the place you are rounding to.

    346   **3**56

2. Look at the digit in the next place, to the right.

    3<u>4</u>6   3<u>5</u>6

3. If the digit in the next place is *4 or less,* **round down:**
    - Do not change the first digit.
    - Change all other digits to zero.

    346 ≈ **300**

4. But if the digit in the next place is *5 or more,* **round up:**
    - Change the first digit to the next higher digit.
    - Change all other digits to zero.

    356 ≈ **400**

Exercise

Copy the numbers in each problem. Then follow the rounding directions on the opposite page and round each number up or down to the nearest place. Follow the example.

1. Round to the nearest ten.
   a. 68
   b. 33
   c. 24
   d. 16

Example: 78

$78 \approx 80$

2. Round to the nearest hundred.
   a. 331
   b. 496
   c. 672
   d. 718

3. Round to the nearest thousand.
   a. 7,670
   b. 2,182
   c. 1,880
   d. 5,409

Rounding to Different Places

A number that fills many places can be rounded to different places. For example, a five-digit number can be rounded to the nearest ten thousand, thousand, hundred, or ten. Here is how the same number can be rounded to two different places.

Example: 32,915

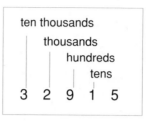

Round to the nearest ten thousand.

1. Find the place to round to.

2. Look at the next digit to the right of the place. If it is 4 or less, *round down*: do not change the digit in the place. Change each digit right of it to 0.

ten thousand

3 2 9 1 5

2 is less than 4, so round down.

3 2̲ 9 1 5 ≈ 3 **0 0 0 0**

Round to the nearest thousand.

1. Find the place to round to.

2. Look at the next digit to the right of the place. If it is 5 or more, *round up*: change the digit in the place to the next higher digit. Change each digit right of it to 0.

thousand

3 **2** 9 1 5

9 is more than 5, so round up.

3 2 9̲ 1 5 ≈ 3 **3 0 0 0**

How would you round 32,915 to the nearest hundred? to the nearest ten?

Exercise

1. Round each number to the thousands place, the hundreds place, and the tens place. Follow the example.

   a. 4,736

   b. 36,151

   c. 2,295

Example: 4,536

4,536 ≈ 5000 thousands place

≈ 4500 hundreds place

≈ 4540 tens place

2. Suppose you save $1,960. Tell *about* how much you have: round to the thousands place, the hundreds place, and the tens place.

Unit 1 Review

Check Yourself

1. List all the digits of our number system.

2. Look at the underlined digit in each number. Write the name of the place that the digit fills.

   a. 2̲4   c. 75̲6   e. 816,0̲49

   b. 1,5̲93   d. 39̲,270   f. 5,14̲3

3. Write the name of the underlined group of places in each number.

   a. 345̲,047,184

   b. 194,736̲,225

   c. 995,700,263̲

4. Copy these numbers and write commas where they belong.

   a. 904   c. 59274   e. 7000000

   b. 58437   d. 13982613   f. 8374

5. Look at the underlined digit in each number. Write the amount that digit stands for.

   a. 27̲   c. 9̲,164   e. 406,2̲87

   b. 3̲98   d. 12,0̲37   f. 1,750̲

6. To show the parts of 38, you write "3 tens and 8 ones." Copy the number below. Then show its parts.

   9,158

7. Copy each amount and regroup it as shown.

   a. 32 ones = ? tens and ? ones

   b. 96 tens = ? hundreds and ? tens

   c. 50 hundreds = ? thousands and ? hundreds

8. Round each number below to the nearest thousand, to the nearest hundred, and to the nearest ten.

   a. 4,715   b. 28,043

9. Copy each sentence and finish it. Use the correct word from this list.

   digits   **regroup**
   places   **round**

   a. A two-digit number fills two ? .

   b. When an amount in a place is more than 9, you ? it.

   c. You ? a number to show an amount that is close to it.

   d. A whole number is made up of ? .

Bonus

1. Find out how a calculator works. Give a demonstration to your class.

2. Make a poster showing the first nine places in a number. (If you need help, look at page 8.)

Subtracting to Compare Amounts

What You Find When You Subtract

Let's say that you are figuring your expenses for the day. You take out all the money you have in your wallet. You count 4 one-dollar bills. You figure these three things.

1. How Much Less

You had more dollars yesterday. You figure how much less you have now. (That is the same as *how much more* you had before.)

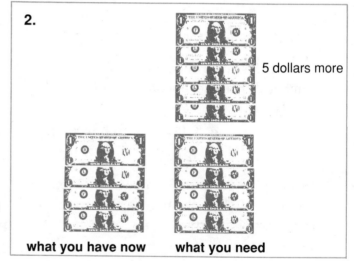

1.

3 dollars more

3 dollars less

what you have now   **what you had before**

2. How Much More

You'd like to buy a shirt. It costs more than you have. You figure how much more money you'd need.

2.

5 dollars more

what you have now   **what you need**

3. How Much Is Left

You decide to buy a ticket for a school event. You figure how much money you will have left.

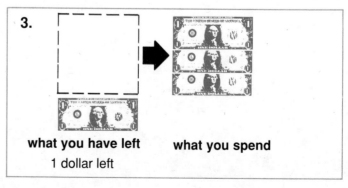

3.

what you have left   **what you spend**
1 dollar left

When you figure your expenses, you are solving real-life math problems. One operation you will do often is subtract one number from another. The answer is the **difference** between the two numbers. You subtract to find:

- *how much more or less* one amount is than another:

    7 dollars **minus 4** dollars **equals 3** dollars

- *how much more you need* to make a larger amount:

    9 dollars **minus 4** dollars **equals 5** dollars

- *how much is left* when you take away an amount:

    4 dollars **minus 3** dollars **equals 1** dollar

You subtract only numbers that stand for the same things. For example, you subtract *dollars* from *dollars*.

Exercise

1. Copy these sentences and finish them. Use the words from this list. Some words will be used more than once.

difference	**more**	**two**
less	**same**	

a. You subtract to find the ___?___ between two amounts.

b. Only numbers that stand for the ___?___ things can be subtracted.

c. You work with ___?___ numbers when you subtract.

d. You find how much ___?___ or ___?___ one amount is than another.

e. You find how much ___?___ you need to make an amount larger.

f. You find how much ___?___ you have when you take away an amount.

2. Look at the items on this list. What items can be subtracted? *Example:* 48 textbooks can be subtracted from 250 textbooks. (Some items can be used more than once.)

1 computer	5 computers
1 deck chair	8 radios
2 computers	10 television sets
2 trucks	20 deck chairs
3 deck chairs	48 textbooks
5 calculators	250 textbooks

21

Lining Up to Subtract

Suppose you have $1,325 in the bank. You want to know how much will be left if you take out $350. To find out you'd subtract. This math sentence tells how:

$1,325 - $350 = ?

To figure the answer to the problem, you must write it as a number problem. You must be careful to **set up** the number problem correctly or you will make a mistake when you subtract. In other words, you must write the numbers so that the digits **line up** in **columns.**

When you line up, you make sure that digits of the same place value are in the same column. You line up ones digits in the same column. You line up tens digits in the same column, and so on.

Here is how the numbers of the problem should line up:

```
 THOUSANDS
    HUNDREDS
       TENS
          ONES
    1  3  2  5
 -     3  5  0
 _____
```

Notice this: the digits 5 and 0 are lined up in the ones column.

What digits are lined up in the tens column?

What digits are lined up in the hundreds column?

What digit is in the thousands column?

Here is how to set up a subtraction problem correctly:

Example: $6{,}298 - 4{,}653 = ?$

1. First write the number to subtract from.

In a math sentence, the number to subtract from is *before* the minus sign. You will use that number to line up the other number. (To help you line up, you can draw lines alongside each column.)

```
6 | 2 | 9 | 8
  |   |   |
```

2. Line up the number that is to be subtracted.

In a math sentence, the number to be subtracted is *after* the minus sign. Line up ones below ones, tens below tens, and so on. Then draw the *minus sign* and the **answer bar**.

```
    6 | 2 | 9 | 8
  - 4 | 6 | 5 | 3
  ─────────────────
      |   |   |
```

> **Remember:**
> − is the *minus sign*. It shows you are subtracting.

3. Make sure each number is copied correctly.

Look at each digit in each number. Make sure each digit is correct.

Now look at the problem.

Which digits are lined up in the ones column? the tens column? the hundreds column? the thousands column?

Which number is larger: the number you *subtract* or the number you *subtract from*?

Exercise

Practice setting up subtraction problems correctly. Line up the numbers in each problem. Then make sure you copied correctly.

1. $397 - 218 = ?$

2. $3{,}038 - 1{,}284 = ?$

3. $827 - 64 = ?$

4. $4{,}967 - 190 = ?$

5. $38{,}174 - 6{,}905 = ?$

6. $792 - 9 = ?$

7. $4{,}026 - 15 = ?$

8. $93{,}106 - 287 = ?$

What Subtraction Facts Do You Know?

When you subtract, you use basic subtraction facts. How many facts do you know? Copy these facts and finish them by writing their answers.

one	two	three	four	five
$1 - 0 =$	$2 - 0 =$	$3 - 0 =$	$4 - 0 =$	$5 - 0 =$
$1 - 1 =$	$2 - 1 =$	$3 - 1 =$	$4 - 1 =$	$5 - 1 =$
	$2 - 2 =$	$3 - 2 =$	$4 - 2 =$	$5 - 2 =$
		$3 - 3 =$	$4 - 3 =$	$5 - 3 =$
			$4 - 4 =$	$5 - 4 =$
				$5 - 5 =$

six	seven	eight	nine	ten
$6 - 0 =$	$7 - 0 =$	$8 - 0 =$	$9 - 0 =$	$10 - 0 =$
$6 - 1 =$	$7 - 1 =$	$8 - 1 =$	$9 - 1 =$	$10 - 1 =$
$6 - 2 =$	$7 - 2 =$	$8 - 2 =$	$9 - 2 =$	$10 - 2 =$
$6 - 3 =$	$7 - 3 =$	$8 - 3 =$	$9 - 3 =$	$10 - 3 =$
$6 - 4 =$	$7 - 4 =$	$8 - 4 =$	$9 - 4 =$	$10 - 4 =$
$6 - 5 =$	$7 - 5 =$	$8 - 5 =$	$9 - 5 =$	$10 - 5 =$
$6 - 6 =$	$7 - 6 =$	$8 - 6 =$	$9 - 6 =$	$10 - 6 =$
	$7 - 7 =$	$8 - 7 =$	$9 - 7 =$	$10 - 7 =$
		$8 - 8 =$	$9 - 8 =$	$10 - 8 =$
			$9 - 9 =$	$10 - 9 =$
				$10 - 10 =$

The Opposite of Subtracting

You subtract to *take away* an amount. You add to *put together* amounts. So, the **opposite** of subtracting is adding. That means: if you subtract to take away an amount, you can add to put it back again.

For example, suppose you start with 7. You subtract 2 and end with 5. See what happens when you add the 5 and the 2:

$$7 - 2 = 5 \qquad 5 + 2 = 7$$

When you add the 5 and the 2, you *add back* to 7. Whenever you subtract, you can add back like that. For example:

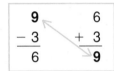 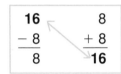 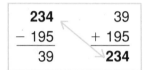

Notice this: to add back, you add the *difference* and the *number that you subtracted*. Your sum will be the *number that you subtracted from*.

Because adding is the opposite of subtracting, you can add to help you subtract correctly. You can add to check your subtraction answers. (You'll learn how in a later lesson.)

Exercise

Copy each problem and fill in the answer. Then add back to the amount you started with.

Example: $9 - 5 = ?$ $9 - 5 = 4$ $4 + 5 = 9$

1. $10 - 8 = ?$ **3.** $8 - 7 = ?$ **5.** $8 - 3 = ?$

2. $6 - 4 = ?$ **4.** $7 - 5 = ?$ **6.** $5 - 3 = ?$

Subtracting Numbers in Parts

Suppose you have $37 in these bills:

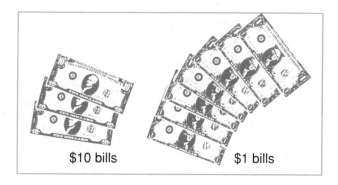

$10 bills $1 bills

3 tens and 7 ones = 37

Then you give away $2.

The amount that you have left is pictured below.
What is the amount?

2 ones

$1 bills

3 tens and 5 ones = 35

$10 bills $1 bills

To find the answer, you count the amount *in parts*:
You count all the $1 bills that are left. And you count the
$10 bills.

When you subtract numbers, you do the same thing: you
figure the answer *in parts*.

For example, suppose you want to subtract to figure the
amount above. You line up the smaller number below the
larger number, like this:

tens	ones
$ 3	7
–	2

3 tens   7 ones
–   2 ones

Then you subtract the numbers in parts: you subtract
ones. And you subtract tens.

To subtract $37 – $2 in parts:

1. Subtract the digits in the ones column.

Subtract the bottom digit from the top digit.

$$
\begin{array}{r}
\$\,3\,7 \\
-\ \ 2 \\
\hline
5
\end{array}
\qquad
\begin{array}{r}
7\ ones \\
-\ 2\ ones \\
\hline
5\ ones
\end{array}
$$

2. Subtract tens.

There is no bottom digit to subtract. So, *bring down* the top digit. It is the answer in the tens column.

$$
\begin{array}{r}
\$\,3\,7 \\
-\ \ 2 \\
\hline
\$\,3\,5
\end{array}
\qquad
\begin{array}{rr}
3\ tens & 7\ ones \\
- & 2\ ones \\
\hline
3\ tens & 5\ ones = 35
\end{array}
$$

The answer shows you have $35 left.

Notice this: to subtract numbers in parts, you subtract digits in columns. You subtract the bottom digit from the top digit. And you work from right to left.

Exercise

1. Count the amount of dollars in this box. Write a subtraction problem with that amount. Show that you subtract 3. Then write the answer.

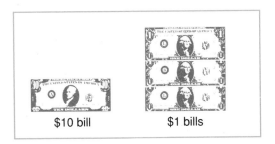

$10 bill $1 bills

2. Line up the numbers in each problem. Then subtract to find the answer.

   a. 49 – 6 = ?   **c.** 57 – 5 = ?

   b. 136 – 4 = ?   **d.** 298 – 3 = ?

Checking Your Answer

To check your subtraction answer, *add back*. In other words, *add* the number you subtracted *back* to the answer. If your subtraction answer is correct, you will end up with the number you subtracted from.

Example:

$$
\begin{array}{r}
3\,8 \\
-\ \ 5 \\
\hline
3\,2 \quad ?
\end{array}
$$

To check the answer, do this: add the answer and the number you subtracted. Compare their sum with the number you subtracted from.

$$
\begin{array}{r}
3\,8 \\
-\ \ 5 \\
\hline
3\,2
\end{array}
\qquad
\begin{array}{r}
3\,2 \\
+\ \ 5 \\
\hline
3\,7
\end{array}
$$

Those numbers should be the same. If they are not, look for a mistake in your work:

1. Look at the way you set up the problem. See if you lined up digits in the wrong column.
2. Look at the way you subtracted. See if you subtracted incorrectly. Also see if you wrote any digits in the wrong column.

In the problem above, something is wrong—37 is not the same as 38. What mistake was made in the problem? What should the correct answer be?

Exercise

Line up the numbers in each problem and subtract. Then add to check each answer. Correct mistakes if you need to.

1. $37 - 4 = ?$ **2.** $68 - 2 = ?$ **3.** $207 - 3 = ?$ **4.** $465 - 3 = ?$

Unit 2 Review

Check Yourself

1. Set up each problem by lining up its numbers correctly. Do not work the problem.

   a. 345 − 3 = ?

   b. 5,974 − 836 = ?

   c. 41,036 − 18,477 = ?

   d. 359,570 − 280,469 = ?

2. Write the missing totals for these problems *without* working the problems.

   a. 9 − 5 = 4, so 4 + 5 = ?

   b. 85 − 46 = 39, so 39 + 46 = ?

   c. 9,476 − 585 = 8,891, so 8,891 + 585 = ?

   d. 45,736 − 29 = 45,707, so 45,707 + 29 = ?

3. Write a number for the amount shown in each box. Then write a subtraction problem to find the difference between the two amounts.

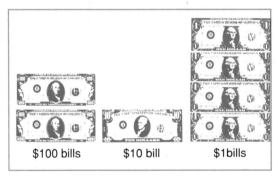

$100 bills $10 bill $1 bills

minus

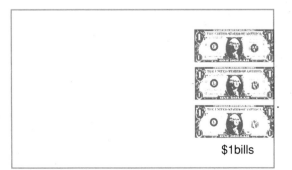

$1 bills

4. Copy each problem below and fill in the answer. Then add back to get to the number you started with.

   a. 18 − 9 = ?   **d.** 12 − 5 = ?

   b. 17 − 8 = ?   **e.** 14 − 7 = ?

   c. 15 − 6 = ?   **f.** 16 − 9 = ?

5. Set up the problems below. Then find the answers and check them.

   a. 49 − 7 = ?   **d.** 8,247 − 2 = ?

   b. 618 − 6 = ?   **e.** 3,505 − 5 = ?

   c. 726 − 3 = ?   **f.** 51,439 − 4 = ?

6. Suppose you work in a store. You have 68 posters to sell. You sell 5 of them. Write a problem showing how many of the posters are left.

7. Copy each sentence and finish it. Use the correct word from this list.

add	difference
larger	minus

   a. The answer to a subtraction problem is called the __?__ .

   b. To check a subtraction answer, you __?__ back.

   c. To set up a subtraction problem, you write the __?__ number first.

   d. You use a __?__ sign to show that you are subtracting.

Bonus

Figure the answer to the question in this *trick* problem:

A farmer had 36 cows. He sold all but 4 of them. How many cows did he have left?

29

Regrouping to Subtract Ones

Regrouping a Ten as Ones

Suppose you have a $10 bill, and you need to give away $7. To do that, you change the $10 bill to ten $1 bills. Then you can give away 7 ones.

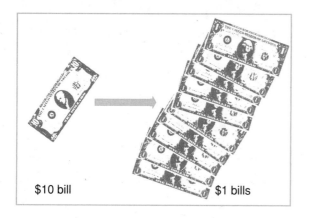

$10 bill $1 bills

You must often do the same thing when you subtract numbers. You change a ten to ones so you can subtract ones. To do that, you *regroup to the right*. You show 1 ten as 10 ones.

For example, suppose you have this problem:

```
tens ones
  3   4          3 tens 4 ones
−     7        −        7 ones
```

Look at the digits in the ones column. You must subtract 7 from 4. But you can't take 7 ones from 4 ones, because 7 is larger than 4.

So, you *regroup* to show more ones. You change 1 ten to 10 ones. You add those 10 ones to the 4 ones. Then you have enough ones to subtract from.

The next page shows what happens when you regroup to the right in the problem.

To regroup ten as ones:

1. Take 1 ten from the tens in the top number.

Cross off the digit in the tens column. Write the next smaller digit above it.

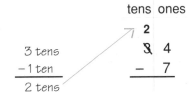

	tens	ones
	2	
3 tens	3̶	4
− 1 ten	−	7
2 tens		

2. Regroup the ten as 10 ones. Add them to the ones digit.

Cross off the top digit in the ones column. Add 10 to that digit and write the total above it.

	tens	ones	
	2	**14**	1 ten = 10 ones
	3̶	4̶	
	−	7	4 ones
			+ 10 ones
			14 ones

To finish the problem, subtract in the ones column. Then bring down the digit in the tens column. What is the answer?

	tens	ones
	2	**14**
	3̶	4̶
−	↓	7
	?	?

2 tens 14 ones
−   7 ones
? tens ? ones

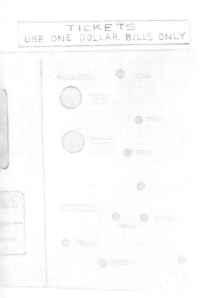

Exercise

1. Copy each problem. Then regroup to show 1 ten as 10 ones. (One is done as an example.)

   a. 2 tens and 3 ones = 1 ten and 13 ones

   b. 6 tens and 7 ones = ?

   c. 1 ten and 5 ones = ?

   d. 5 tens and 4 ones = ?

2. Regroup: Show 1 ten as 10 ones. Then subtract. (The first problem is started.)

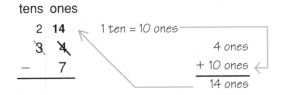

   2 17

a. 3̶ 7̶   **b.** 85   **c.** 96   **d.** 23
 − 9   − 8   − 9   − 6

31

Regrouping Again to Show Ones

Suppose you must subtract this problem:

$$102$$
$$-5$$
$$\overline{?}$$

To subtract the ones digit, you must regroup 1 ten as 10 ones. The picture at right shows what 102 stands for. Notice this: there are no tens in the tens place, so there is no ten to regroup.

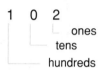

1 hundred   0 tens   2 ones

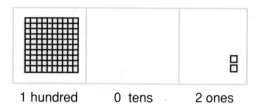

When 0 is in the tens place, you must do this: regroup 1 hundred as 10 tens.

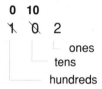

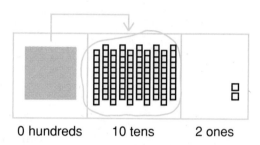

0 hundreds   10 tens   2 ones

Now there are 0 hundreds and 10 tens and 2 ones. You can regroup *1 ten as 10 ones:*

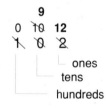

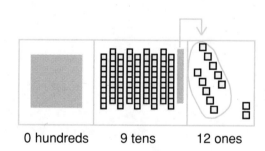

0 hundreds   9 tens   12 ones

There are now 0 hundreds and 9 tens and 12 ones.

How many times did you regroup to show more ones in 102? What did you regroup first? What did you regroup next?

You regrouped two times. First, you regrouped
1 hundred as 10 tens like this:

Next, you regrouped 1 ten as 10 ones like
this:

Exercise

Regroup each number to show more ones.
Follow the example.

1. 403

2. 605

3. 207

4. 107

5. 303

6. 104

7. 505

8. 902

Regrouping Two Times to Subtract Ones

You learned how to regroup two times to show more ones in a number. You will need to do that in problems like this:

Example:

$$
\begin{array}{r}
4\ 0\ 7 \\
-\quad\ \ 9 \\
\hline
\end{array}
$$

1. Regroup 1 hundred as 10 tens.

Take 1 hundred from the hundreds column and regroup it as tens. Add the regrouped tens to the digit in the tens column.

4 hundreds	3 10	0 tens
− 1 hundred	4 0 7	+ 10 tens
3 hundreds	− 9	10 tens

2. Regroup 1 ten as 10 ones.

Take 1 ten from the tens column and regroup it as ones. Add the regrouped ones to the digit in the ones column.

10 tens	9	7 ones
− 1 ten	3 10 17	+ 10 ones
9 tens	4 0 7	17 ones
	− 9	

Look back at the top number in the problem. How many hundreds are there now? How many tens? How many ones?

Now you can subtract to find the difference between 407 and 9. Subtract in the ones column. Bring down the digit in the tens and hundreds columns.

$$
\begin{array}{r}
9 \\
3\ \ 10\ 17 \\
4\ 0\ 7 \\
-\downarrow\ \downarrow\ 9 \\
\hline
3\ 9\ 8
\end{array}
$$

Notice this: when you must regroup to subtract, you regroup from left to right. And you regroup one step at a time—from one column to the next.

> **Remember:**
> To show more ones in a number, regroup 1 ten as 10 ones.
> If 0 fills the tens place, *first* regroup 1 hundred as 10 tens.

Exercise

1. Line up the numbers in each problem. Regroup to show more ones, then subtract. (Be sure to check your answers.)

    a. 302 − 4 = ?   **d.** 806 − 8 = ?

    b. 405 − 9 = ?   **e.** 903 − 7 = ?

    c. 504 − 8 = ?   **f.** 600 − 2 = ?

2. Read these word problems. Write them as number problems and solve them.

    a. Football player Ozzie Newsome caught 502 passes in his career. Ahmad Rashad caught 7 fewer passes. How many passes did Rashad catch?

    b. In 1986, baseball player Wade Boggs made 107 runs. His teammate Jim Rice made 9 fewer runs. How many runs did Rice make?

Regrouping to the Right

Sometimes you will have to regroup several times before you can subtract. You do the same thing each time: take away 1 from one place. Regroup the 1 as 10. Add the 10 to the next place at right.

Example: 3,004 − 9

1. Regroup 1 thousand as 10 hundreds.

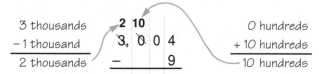

3 thousands	0 hundreds
− 1 thousand	+ 10 hundreds
2 thousands	10 hundreds

2. Regroup 1 hundred as 10 tens.

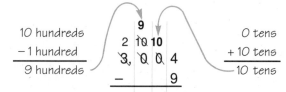

10 hundreds	0 tens
− 1 hundred	+ 10 tens
9 hundreds	10 tens

3. Regroup 1 ten as 10 ones.

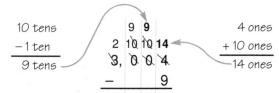

10 tens	4 ones
− 1 ten	+ 10 ones
9 tens	14 ones

The problem can now be subtracted:

```
      9  9
  2  10 10 14
  3,  0  0  4
 −  ↓  ↓  ↓  9
  2, 9  9  5
```

Notice this: to show more ones in a number, you first find the *closest place that is not filled with 0.* You start regrouping from that place.

Now use what you learned. On notepaper, line up this problem:

$$
\begin{array}{r}
6,005 \\
-6 \\
\hline
\end{array}
$$

Then answer these questions about it:

1. Why must you regroup before you subtract ones?
2. What place do you regroup from first?
3. How many times do you need to regroup to show more ones?
4. What is the answer to the problem?

Exercise

1. Line up the numbers in each problem and subtract.
   Regroup where you need to. Then check your answers.

   a. 3,001 − 5 = ?   **d.** 8,008 − 9 = ?

   b. 1,005 − 6 = ?   **e.** 1,404 − 7 = ?

   c. 2,000 − 6 = ?   **f.** 4,003 − 7 = ?

2. Read the word problem. Write it as a number problem
   and solve it.

   Suppose the goal for your school fundraiser was
   $2,000. The school raised $8 less than that. How
   much did your school raise?

Subtracting to Compare Sales

This graph is a double line graph. It shows two sets of amounts so you can compare them. One set of amounts is shown by dots along the thick black line. The other set of amounts is shown by dots along the thin black line.

The graph shows how many tickets two different workers sold during a 5-day week. The thick black line shows the sales of worker A. The thin black line shows the sales of worker B.

Look at the colored lines that go across the graph. Each line stands for a number of tickets. That number is shown at the beginning of the line.

Look at the colored lines that go down the graph. Each line stands for a day. That day is shown at the bottom of the graph.

Now look at the dots. Each dot is placed where two colored lines meet. So, each dot shows how many tickets were sold by worker A or B on a day of the week.

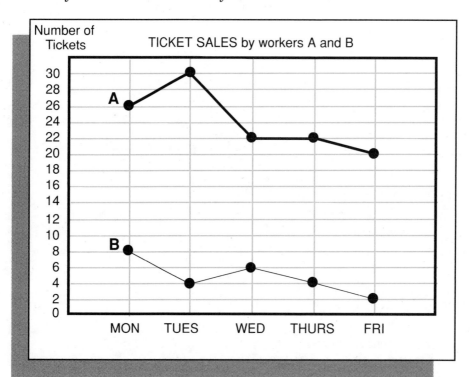

Find the dot that stands for the sales of worker A on Monday. It shows that worker A sold 26 tickets. Find the dot that stands for the sales of worker B on Monday. How many tickets did worker B sell?

Suppose you want to compare the sales of both workers on Monday. The graph shows that worker A sold more tickets than worker B. To find how much more, you subtract:

$$26 - 8 = ? \text{ tickets difference}$$

How many more tickets did worker A sell on Monday?

Exercise

Use the graph to answer the questions.

1. On Tuesday, how many
   a. tickets did worker A sell?
   b. tickets did worker B sell?
   c. more tickets did worker A sell than worker B?

2. On Wednesday, how many
   a. tickets did worker A sell?
   b. tickets did worker B sell?
   c. more tickets did worker A sell than worker B?

3. Find the day when *both* workers sold the *fewest* tickets:
   a. What day was it?
   b. How many tickets did worker A sell that day?
   c. How many tickets did worker B sell that day?
   d. How many *more* tickets did worker A sell than worker B on that day?

Unit 3 Review

Check Yourself

1. Answer the questions below the pictures.

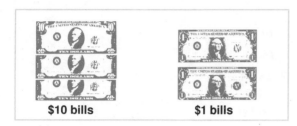

$10 bills $1 bills

If you change a ten to ones, how many

a. tens will be left?

b. ones will there be now?

$100 bills

If you change a hundred to tens, how many

c. hundreds will be left?

d. tens will there be now?

2. Copy each amount and regroup it to show more ones in the ones column. Follow the example.

> **Example:** 8|0|3   9
>   7 ₁₀ 13
>   8̶ 0̶ 3̶

a. 9|6   **d.** 5|0|7

b. 8|0   **e.** 2|0|4

c. 4|9|1   **f.** 1|0|0|0

3. Set up the problems below. Then find the answers and check them.

a. $68 - 9 = ?$ **e.** $178 - 8 = ?$

b. $545 - 7 = ?$ **f.** $2{,}234 - 5 = ?$

c. $204 - 6 = ?$ **g.** $706 - 3 = ?$

d. $1{,}003 - 4 = ?$ **h.** $5{,}000 - 2 = ?$

4. To complete each sentence below, choose the correct word from this list:

> bottom   hundred   ten   top

a. In a subtraction problem, you must subtract the __?__ number from the other number.

b. To show more ones in a number, you regroup a __?__ .

c. You regroup only in the __?__ number of a subtraction problem.

d. To show more tens in a number, you regroup a __?__ .

Bonus

1. Find out how to use an abacus to work this subtraction problem:

$$200 - 5 = ?$$

Then show the class how to do it.

2. Design a counting machine that you could use (like an abacus) to add or subtract with. Make or draw your machine. Then show the class how to use it.

Subtracting Larger Numbers

Subtracting a Two-Digit Number

Suppose you have a job printing posters. You must print 70 posters. You print 26 of them. How many more must you print? To find out, you subtract with two-digit numbers:

$$\begin{array}{r} 7\ 0 \\ -\ 2\ 6 \\ \hline \end{array}$$

1. Subtract in the ones column.

There are no ones to subtract from. So you must first regroup a ten as ones.

$$\begin{array}{r} 7\ tens \\ -\ 1\ tens \\ \hline 6\ tens \end{array} \qquad \begin{array}{r} ^{6}\,^{10} \\ \not{7}\ \not{0} \\ -\ 2\ \mathbf{6} \\ \hline \mathbf{4} \end{array} \qquad \begin{array}{r} 0\ ones \\ +\ 10\ ones \\ \hline 10\ ones \end{array}$$

2. Subtract in the tens column.

$$\begin{array}{r} ^{6}\ ^{10} \\ \not{7}\ \not{0} \\ -\ 2\ 6 \\ \hline \mathbf{4}\ 4 \end{array} \quad \text{more posters}$$

After you regroup, how many ones do you subtract from? How many tens do you subtract?

Why do you think it is important to cross off digits when you regroup?

Exercise

1. Line up the numbers in each problem and subtract. Regroup when needed. Check your answers.

   a. 42 − 26 = ?   **d.** 88 − 39 = ?
   b. 76 − 33 = ?   **e.** 71 − 62 = ?
   c. 94 − 53 = ?   **f.** 53 − 48 = ?

2. Read this word problem. Write it as a number problem and solve it.

   Suppose you have 36 pencils. You sell 18 of them. How many pencils do you have left?

41

Subtracting Many-digit Numbers

You can subtract numbers of any size if you use what you learned about subtracting in columns:

- Line up digits correctly in columns.
- Subtract in each column, one at a time.
- Work from right to left, starting with the ones column.

For example, suppose you are subtracting with three-digit numbers. That means you subtract in three columns. You start with the ones column. Which column do you end with? (Hint: Look at the picture at the right.)

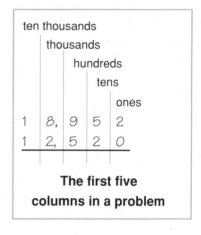

The first five columns in a problem

```
       start here
         ↓
       7 4 6
     − 2 1 5
     ─────────
       5 3 1
```

Now look at this problem:

```
         start here
           ↓
     1 8, 9 5 2
   − 1 2, 5 2 0
   ─────────────
```

How many columns do you subtract in? Which column do you start with? Which do you end with?

Line up the problem on notepaper and find the answer. Then add back to see if it is correct. Fix any mistakes you find.

Exercise

1. Copy each problem. Subtract and check.

  a.   864
      − 343

  c.   426
      − 204

  e.   2,398
      − 1,188

  b.   9,864
      − 9,743

  d. 59,426
      − 21,204

  f.   23,985
      − 21,882

2. Read this word problem. Write it as a number problem and solve it.

The score of a basketball game was Bulls 147, Pistons 123. How many points did the Bulls win by?

Deciding When to Regroup

You will sometimes have to subtract from a number with many digits, so you will subtract in many columns. But you will not be able to subtract in *any* column if the top digit in it is smaller than the bottom digit. Before you can subtract, you will have to regroup.

For example, look at the columns in problem A. You can subtract ones. You can subtract tens. But you *can't* subtract hundreds until you regroup. Why is that so?

The top digit (5) in the hundreds column is smaller than the bottom digit (9). So, you must show more hundreds to subtract from. You regroup 1 thousand as 10 hundreds.

Now look at problem B. Look at each column, from right to left. Find the first column where you can't subtract until you regroup. Then answer these questions:

1. Which column has a top digit that is smaller than the bottom digit?

2. What is the top digit? What is the bottom digit?

3. What do you regroup? How do you regroup it?

A.
thousands
  hundreds
    tens
      ones

```
  3,5 4 8
− 1,9 3 6
```

B.
ten thousands
  thousands
    hundreds
      tens
        ones

```
  7 5,2 5 3
− 3 8,0 4 3
```

Exercise

Copy each problem.

a. Name the first column where you must regroup before you subtract.

b. Tell what you regroup and how. Follow the example.

1.	**2.**	**3.**
274	7,251	88,356
− 129	− 3,831	− 39,072

Example:

```
    3 2 4
  − 1 3 2
```

a. Regroup to subtract in the tens column.

b. Regroup 1 hundred as 10 tens.

Regrouping as You Subtract

You will sometimes have to regroup many times as you work a problem.

Example: $8,672 - 1,681 = ?$

1. Subtract ones.

```
  8, 6 7 2
- 1, 6 8 1
_____
          1
```

2. Subtract tens.

The top digit (7) is smaller than the bottom digit (8). You must regroup to show more tens.

6 hundreds   **5 17**   7 tens
− 1 hundred   8, 6̶ 7̶ 2   + 10 tens
_____   − 1, 6 8 1   _____
5 hundreds   9 1   17 tens

3. Subtract hundreds.

The top hundreds digit is now *smaller* than the bottom digit. You must regroup to show more hundreds.

8 thousands   **15**   5 hundreds
                    7 5̶ 17
− 1 thousand   8, 6̶ 7̶ 2   + 10 hundreds
_____   − 1, 6 8 1   _____
7 thousands   9 9 1   15 hundreds

4. Subtract thousands.

```
        15
    7   5 17
  8, 6 7 2
− 1, 6 8 1
_____
  6, 9 9 1
```

Exercise

1. Copy each problem. (Make sure you copy correctly.) Subtract, regrouping when you need to. Then check your answers.

   a. 747 − 653 = ?

   b. 7,546 − 2,378 = ?

   c. 9,368 − 3,599 = ?

   d. 2,803 − 2,683 = ?

   e. 51,834 − 26,195 = ?

   f. 73,518 − 43,699 = ?

2. Read the word problem. Write it as a math problem and solve it.

   You are reporting on the planets. You read that the diameter of Jupiter is 88,732 miles. The diameter of Earth is 7,926 miles. How much larger is Jupiter's diameter?

3. Think about it: Suppose you subtract digits in four columns. Will your answer ever fill *fewer* than four places? Will it ever fill *more* than four places? Why do you think so?

Regrouping over Zeros

When you subtract numbers with many digits you may need to regroup *over zero*. That happens when the number you subtract from has 0 in it and you need to regroup more than once to subtract in a column.

Example:

$$
\begin{array}{r}
3,0\,6\,8 \\
-\ 1,2\,9\,4 \\
\hline
4
\end{array}
$$

Before you can subtract tens, you must regroup to show more tens. But 0 fills the hundreds place. So, you must regroup *two times:* First, regroup 1 thousand as 10 hundreds.

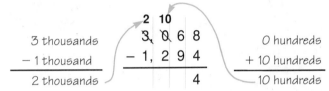

3 thousands
− 1 thousand
2 thousands

0 hundreds
+ 10 hundreds
10 hundreds

Then regroup 1 hundred as 10 tens.

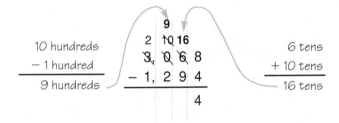

10 hundreds
− 1 hundred
9 hundreds

6 tens
+ 10 tens
16 tens

Now you can subtract tens and finish the problem. What is the answer?

Exercise

1. Line up each problem. Subtract, regrouping when you need to. Then check your answers.
   a. 5,024 − 2,271 = ?
   b. 5,007 − 3,455 = ?
   c. 30,065 − 10,791 = ?
   d. 20,604 − 19,416 = ?

2. Read this word problem. Then write it as a number problem and solve it.

   Suppose you want to buy a car. One car costs $2,000. An older car costs $1,180. How much money will you save if you buy the older car?

When Numbers Fill Different Places

In a subtraction problem, the top number sometimes has more digits than the bottom number. In other words, some columns will have two digits and some will have only one.

Example:

```
  2, 0 0 0
 −     8 9
```

To finish that problem, you need to *bring down* the digits in the hundreds and thousands columns as answers.

It's easy to forget to bring down digits. So, here's how you can write those kinds of problems to help make sure you finish them:

First, line up the numbers in columns. Fill out the bottom number: write a zero under each top digit that should be brought down. The bottom number will then have as many digits as the top number. How many digits will each column now have?

```
  2, 0 0 0
 − 0 0 8 9
```

Now copy the problem. Be sure to fill out the bottom number by writing zeros. Then solve the problem. What is the answer?

Exercise

Line up the numbers for each problem. Fill out the bottom number by writing zeros. Subtract the problem and check your answer. Follow the example.

a. $856 - 7 = ?$

b. $923 - 14 = ?$

c. $4,372 - 95 = ?$

d. $62,043 - 246 = ?$

e. $6,275 - 284 = ?$

f. $24,825 - 68 = ?$

Example: $421 - 35 = ?$

```
       11
   3  ⅟  11
   4  2  1
 − 0  3  5
   3  8  6
```

```
     1  1
   3  8  6
 + 0  3  5
   4  2  1   check
```

Subtracting to Compare Distances

You can use a *road map* to compare distances. For example, you can compare distances between different towns. And you can compare different *routes* to the same town.

Look at the *legend* on the map below. It shows that the thin lines on the map stand for roads and the thick lines stand for highways (hwy).

Some towns are connected only by road. Some are connected only by highway. And some are connected by both. For example, find Rye and Dodd on the map. The distance between them is 153 miles by road. How many miles is it by highway?

The distance between Rye and Dodd is 136 miles by highway. Now suppose you want to find how much shorter the highway route is than the road route. Then you subtract: 153 − 136 = ? miles. What is the answer?

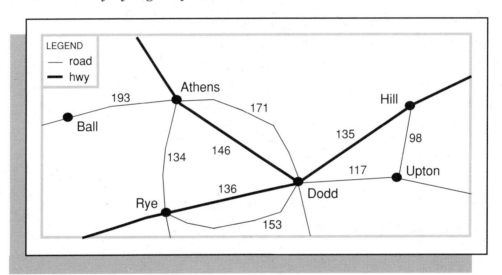

Exercise

Use the map to answer these questions. (Then check your answers.)

1. Find Dodd, Upton, Ball, and Athens.
   a. How many miles is it from Dodd to Upton?
   b. How many miles is it from Ball to Athens?
   c. Which is shorter: Dodd to Upton or Ball to Athens? How much shorter?

2. Find Hill, Upton, and Dodd.
   a. How many miles is it from Hill to Upton?
   b. How many miles is it from Hill to Dodd?
   c. Which is shorter: Hill to Upton or Hill to Dodd? How much shorter?

3. Find Athens and Dodd.
   a. How many miles is it from Athens to Dodd by road?
   b. How many miles is it from Athens to Dodd by highway?
   c. How much shorter is the highway route?

Unit 4 Review

Check Yourself

1. Look at the problems below. For each shaded column, tell why you must regroup before you subtract.

   a.   48,279
          – 32,354

   b. 2,028
        – 416

2. Copy this problem and solve it. Then answer the questions about it.

        4,035
      – 1,062

  a. Which column did you subtract in first?

  b. Which column did you subtract in last?

  c. In one column, you could not subtract until you regrouped. Which column was it?

  d. Which column did you regroup *from* first?

3. Set up each problem below. Then subtract. Check your answers.

  a. 72 – 58 = ?

  b. 976 – 647 = ?

  c. 403 – 296 = ?

  d. 1,582 – 1,496 = ?

  e. 3,042 – 2,273 = ?

  f. 50,021 – 21,460 = ?

  g. 60,503 – 19,315 = ?

  h. 4,057 – 1,183 = ?

4. Set up each problem below. In the bottom number of each problem, write zeros so that each column has two digits. Then subtract. Check your answers.

  a. 385 – 47 = ?

  b. 6,796 – 29 = ?

  c. 1,274 – 435 = ?

  d. 32,732 – 84 = ?

  e. 21,664 – 431 = ?

5. Read each word problem and write it as a number problem. Solve the problem and check your answer.

  a. You have 35 offices to clean. You clean 17 of them. How many more do you have to clean?

  b. In the United States, 389,230 girls played high school basketball in 1984. In the same year, 75,944 girls played soccer. How many more girls played basketball than soccer?

Bonus

Make up some subtraction problems for your class. Find team *statistics* about a sport that you like. For example, find a list that shows how many points each player on a basketball team scored in a season.

Think up five subtraction problems that compare some of the statistics. Write the statistics and the problems on poster board. Write the answers on the back of the poster board.

Estimating Differences

Figuring <u>about</u> What a Difference Is

Imagine this:

- You are in a store. You want to know *about how much money* you will have left after you buy something at the store.

- You are in class. You wonder *about how many minutes* more the class period will be.

- You are at a football game. You want to know *about how many points* one team is ahead of the other.

Those are examples of a kind of subtraction problem you solve often in real life. You don't need an *exact answer* for that kind of problem. You just need an **estimate**—an idea of *about how much* a difference should be.

Estimating can also help find an *exact* answer. If you estimate *before* you work a problem, you'll have an idea of what the correct answer should be. Then, if you get an answer that is very different, you'll know that you figured incorrectly.

So, always estimate before you work a subtraction problem with paper and pencil. And always estimate before you subtract numbers on a calculator.

Exercise

Write each sentence and fill in the missing round number. Follow the directions after the sentence.

1. The Lincoln Tunnel is about __?__ feet long.　**(Round 8,216 to the thousands place.)**

2. A giraffe can run about __?__ miles per hour.　**(Round 32 to the tens place.)**

3. There are about __?__ calories in a milkshake.　**(Round 355 to the <u>tens place</u>.)**

Estimating with Two-Digit Numbers

Suppose you go shopping with $42. You find something you want for $18. Before you buy it, you want to know *about* how much money you will have left. Here is how to estimate the difference between two-digit numbers.

$42 - $18 = ? dollars

1. Round each number to the nearest ten.

42 ≈ **40**

18 ≈ **20**

2. Subtract with the rounded tens.

$$\begin{array}{r} \$4\,0 \\ -\ 2\,0 \\ \hline \$2\,0 \end{array}$$ estimate

The estimate shows that the difference between 42 and 18 is *about* 20. To find the exact difference between 42 and 18, you'd subtract the exact numbers. Now, see how close the answer is to the estimate.

$$\begin{array}{r} \$4\,0 \\ -\ 2\,0 \\ \hline \$2\,0 \end{array}$$ estimate $$\begin{array}{r} {\scriptstyle 3\ 12} \\ \$4\,\not2 \\ -\ 1\,8 \\ \hline \$2\,4 \end{array}$$ answer

---

To Round to the Nearest Ten

1. Look at the digit in the ones place.

    42   18

2. Round down if that digit is 4 or less.

    42 ≈ **40**

3. Round up if that digit is 5 or more.

    18 ≈ **20**

Remember: ≈ means *is about equal to.*

Exercise

1. For each problem, round the numbers and estimate the difference. Then subtract exact numbers and find the answer. Follow the example.

   a. 58 − 29 = ?   **c.** 37 − 11 =?   **e.** 29 − 17 = ?

   b. 92 − 65 = ?   **d.** 67 − 32 =?   **f.** 85 − 46 = ?

   Example: 68 − 39 = ?

   $$\begin{array}{r} 70 \\ -\ 40 \\ \hline 30 \end{array}$$ estimate $$\begin{array}{r} {\scriptstyle 5\ 18} \\ \not6\not8 \\ -\ 39 \\ \hline 29 \end{array}$$ answer

2. Suppose this was the score of a football game: Cleveland 42, Pittsburgh 14. Estimate to find *about* how much Cleveland won by.

Estimating with Larger Numbers

You'll sometimes want to estimate the difference between larger numbers. If both numbers *fill the same places*, you round each of them to the place farthest left.

Example: $2,198 − $1,272 = ? dollars

1. Round numbers to the place farthest left.

The place farthest left in the example is the thousands place.

thousands place   2,198 ≈ **2,000**
                      1,272 ≈ **1,000**

2. Subtract with the rounded numbers.

$$\begin{array}{r} \$\,2,000 \\ -\ 1,000 \\ \hline \$\,1,000 \end{array} \text{ estimate}$$

The difference between $2,198 and $1,272 is about $1,000. Now, copy the problem on notepaper. Find the exact difference. What is it?

$$\begin{array}{r} \$\,2,000 \\ -\ 1,000 \\ \hline \$\,1,000 \end{array} \text{ estimate} \qquad \begin{array}{r} \$\,2,198 \\ -\ 1,272 \\ \hline \$\quad ? \end{array} \text{ answer}$$

To Round to the Place Farthest Left

1. Look at the digit in the place farthest left.
       2,918   **1,272**

2. If the *next* digit is 5 or more, round *up*.
       2,918 ≈ **3,000**

3. But if the next digit is 4 or less, round *down*.
               1,272 ≈ **1,000**

Exercise

1. For each problem, round the numbers and estimate the difference. Then subtract exact numbers and find the answer. Follow the example.

   a. 397 − 125 = ?

   b. 934 − 798 = ?

   c. 8,164 − 6,325 = ?

   d. 4,207 − 2,916 = ?

   e. 59,425 − 26,201 = ?

   f. 51,826 − 36,410 = ?

   > **Example:** 488 − 225 = ?
   >
   > $$\begin{array}{r} 500 \\ -\ 200 \\ \hline 300 \end{array}\ \text{estimate}\qquad \begin{array}{r} 488 \\ -\ 225 \\ \hline 263 \end{array}\ \text{answer}$$

2. Suppose your team has 425 candy bars to sell. You sell 187. Estimate to find *about* how many you still have to sell.

3. To rent a house would cost you $11,220 a year. To rent an apartment would cost you $7,776 a year. Estimate the difference in the costs for both places.

When Numbers Fill Different Places

Sometimes, you need to estimate the difference between numbers that do not fill all the same places. To do that, you round *both* numbers to the same place.

Example: 3,287 − 925 = ?

1. Find the largest place that *both* numbers fill.

That place is the one that is farthest left in the *smaller number*.

hundreds place   3,287
              925

2. Round both numbers to that place.

In the example, both numbers are rounded to the hundreds place.

hundreds place   3,287 ≈ **3,300** (33 hundreds)
           925 ≈   **900** (9 hundreds)

3. Subtract with the rounded numbers.

```
    2  13
   3, 3 0 0
 − 0 9 0 0
 ─────────
   2, 4 0 0  estimate
```

The difference between 3,287 and 925 is *about* 2,400. Now copy the problem on notepaper. Find the *exact* difference. What is it?

```
   3, 3 0 0              3, 2 8 7
 − 0 9 0 0            − 0 9 2 5
 ─────────            ─────────
   2, 4 0 0  estimate       ?    answer
```

To Round to the Same Place

1. Find the place in both numbers.
     3,287   925

2. If the *next* digit is 5 or more, round *up*.
     3,287 ≈ **3,300**

3. But if the next digit is 4 or less, round *down*.
          925 ≈ **900**

Exercise

1. For each problem, round the numbers and subtract to find the estimate. Then use the exact numbers and subtract to find the answer. (Follow the example.)

   a. 257 − 68 = ?

   b. 3,864 − 219 = ?

   c. 8,317 − 72 = ?

   d. 726 − 41 = ?

   e. 4,917 − 346 = ?

   f. 5,508 − 64 = ?

Example: 156 − 32 = ?	
160	156
− 030	− 32
130 estimate	124 answer

2. Texas covers 267,338 acres. Rhode Island covers only 1,214 acres. Estimate *about* how much larger Texas is than Rhode Island.

3. You need $12,198 to buy a car. You have saved $935 so far. Estimate how much more you must save.

Comparing Estimates and Answers: Tens

Suppose you estimate a difference by using round tens. Then you subtract exact numbers to find the answer. If your answer is correct, it will be close to the estimate. Here is how to see if the answer and estimate are close:

Example:

$$
\begin{array}{r}
9\,0 \\
-\ 6\,0 \\
\hline
3\,0
\end{array}
\text{ estimate}
\qquad
\begin{array}{r}
8\,7 \\
-\ 6\,4 \\
\hline
2\,3
\end{array}
\text{ answer ?}
$$

1. **In the estimate:** Circle the tens in the estimate.

2. **In the answer:** Circle the tens in the answer.

3. **Compare:** Subtract the smaller tens from the larger tens. If the difference is 1 or 0, your answer probably is close to the estimate. If the difference is 2 or more, the answer probably is not close to the estimate.

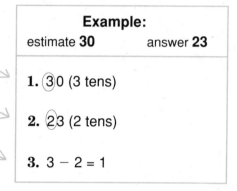

Example:

estimate **30**   answer **23**

1. ③0 (3 tens)

2. ②3 (2 tens)

3. 3 − 2 = 1

Is 30 close to 23? Why do you say so?

Exercise

Copy each estimate and answer.
Then compare them. Write **close** or **not
close**, and give your reason. Follow the
example.

1. estimate = 30
   answer = 37

2. estimate = 40
   answer = 61

3. estimate = 60
   answer = 52

4. estimate = 90
   answer = 92

5. estimate = 10
   answer = 21

6. estimate = 70
   answer = 92

Example: estimate = 50   (5)0
            answer = 73   (7)3

$$\begin{array}{r} 7 \\ -\ 5 \\ \hline 2 \end{array}$$ not close because
2 is more than 1

Comparing Larger Estimates and Answers

Here is how you can compare estimates and answers when you are working with larger numbers, such as in this problem:

$$
\begin{array}{r}
\overset{3\;17}{\cancel{4},\cancel{8}\,0\,0} \\
-\quad 9\,0\,0 \\
\hline
3,8\,0\,0 \text{ estimate}
\end{array}
\qquad
\begin{array}{r}
\overset{3\;16\;4\;11}{\cancel{4},\cancel{8}\,\cancel{5}\,\cancel{1}} \\
-\quad 9\,2\,7 \\
\hline
3,7\,2\,4 \text{ answer ?}
\end{array}
$$

1. **In the estimate:** Find the place you rounded to. Circle the amount that has its place value.

2. **In the answer:** Circle the amount that has the same place value.

3. **Compare:** Subtract the smaller circled amount from the larger circled amount. If the difference is 1 or 0, your answer probably is close. If the difference is 2 or more, the answer probably is not close to the estimate.

Is 3,800 close to 3,724? Why do you say so?

Example:

estimate **3,800**　　　answer **3,724**

1. ③,⑧0 0 (38 hundreds)

2. ③,⑦2 4 (37 hundreds)

3. 3 8 − 3 7 = 1

Exercise

The circled amounts in each estimate show the place that was rounded to. Copy the estimate and the answer.

Then compare them. Write **close** or **not close** and give your reason. Follow the example.

Example: estimate = 500 ⑤0 0
answer = 821 ⑧2 1

```
  8
− 5
  3  not close because
     3 is more than 1
```

1. estimate = ③00
answer = 293

2. estimate = ①00
answer = 415

3. estimate = ⑦0,000
answer = 67,843

4. estimate = ①,500
answer = 1,476

5. estimate = ②,500
answer = 1,983

6. estimate = ①,640
answer = 2,352

If Your Answer Is Not Close

Suppose you have this problem:

$613 - 187 = ?$

You use round hundreds to estimate the difference.
You then subtract the exact numbers to find the answer.
And you compare your answer with your estimate.

```
                           10
                        2  8 16
 613 ≈   6 0 0          8  1 8        ④0 0     4
 187 ≈ – 2 0 0        – 1  8 7        ①2 9   – 1
        ———————                      ——————
         4 0 0  estimate  1 2 9  answer?       3  not close
```

The answer is not close to the estimate. That means you have
made a mistake. Here is how to find that mistake.

1. Look at your estimate.

Did you use the correct numbers? Did you round up or down
correctly? Did you subtract correctly?

2. Look at the actual problem.

Did you line up correctly? Did you subtract and regroup
correctly? Did you write digits in the correct column?

Now look back at the problem. Copy it on notepaper. Then
find what is wrong and fix it. Compare your new answer and
estimate.

What was wrong with the problem?

Exercise

Copy each problem. Find out why the answer is not close to
the estimate. Fix any mistakes. Then compare again. Make sure
the answer is close to the estimate.

1. $48 - 29 = ?$

```
     50              48
   – 30            – 29
   ————            ————
     20  estimate    59  answer?
```

2. $73 - 16 = ?$

```
     70              73
   – 20            – 61
   ————            ————
     50  estimate    12  answer?
```

If Your Answer Is Close

Suppose you find an exact answer that *is* close to your estimate when you subtract. For example:

```
 528 ≈  5 0 0          5 2 8         4 0 0    4
 132 ≈ -1 0 0         -1 3 2         4 1 6  - 4
        ─────                ─────              ───
        4 0 0 estimate   4 1 6 answer ?        0 close
```

Does the estimate prove the answer is correct?

No. The estimate shows that the answer *makes sense*. To see if it is exactly correct, you must check it. You learned to add back to do that:

```
 5 2 8           4 1 6
-1 3 2          +1 3 2
 ─────           ─────
 4 1 6           5 4 8 check
```

The sum you find should be the same as the number you subtracted from. In the problem above, it is *not* the same. So, something is wrong. To find the mistake, look for:

- digits that are copied wrong.
- digits that are lined up wrong.
- digits that are written in the wrong column.
- incorrect subtracting in the problem.
- incorrect adding in the check.

What is the mistake in the problem above? What is the correct answer?

Exercise

1. For each problem, first estimate the difference. Next, find the exact answer. Then compare and check the answer and the estimate. Find and fix any mistakes.

   a. 58 − 23 = ?   **b.** 921 − 675 = ?   **c.** 2,367 − 1,516 = ?

2. Suppose you are going to pay $1,249 for a motorbike. You pay $525 right away. Estimate to see *about* what amount you still owe. Then find the *exact* amount. Compare the answer and estimate and check your answer. Find and fix any mistakes.

Estimating to Compare Salaries

Sooner or later, you will decide on a *career* for yourself. Before you do, you may want to compare how much money you would make on different jobs.

The *bar graph* on this page shows the salaries for certain jobs. You can use the graph to compare the salaries. Taller bars on the graph stand for higher salaries. Shorter bars stand for lower salaries. (The exact salaries are written above the bars.)

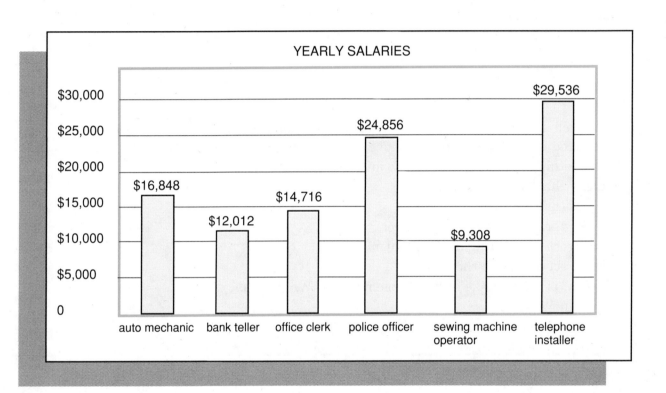

YEARLY SALARIES

Find the bar that stands for the salary of a *telephone installer*. What is that salary?

Now find the salary of a *bank teller*. What is it?

The graph shows that a telephone installer's salary ($29,536) is more than a bank teller's salary ($12,012). *About* how much more is it?

To find out, estimate the difference: Round the numbers to ten thousands and subtract:

$$\begin{array}{rcr} \$\,29{,}536 & \approx & \$\,3\,0{,}0\,0\,0 \\ \$\,12{,}012 & \approx & -\,\$\,1\,0{,}0\,0\,0 \\ \hline & & \$\qquad ? \end{array}$$

What is the estimate?

Exercise

Find the salaries for each pair of jobs listed below. Use the graph to find the answers. Estimate the difference. Then find the exact difference. (Compare and check.)

1. auto mechanic and police officer
   a. salaries = ? and ?
   b. estimate = ?
   c. exact difference = ?

2. bank teller and office clerk
   a. salaries = ? and ?
   b. estimate = ?
   c. exact difference = ?

3. police officer and telephone installer
   a. salaries = ? and ?
   b. estimate = ?
   c. exact difference = ?

4. sewing machine operator and auto mechanic
   a. salaries = ? and ?
   b. estimate = ?
   c. exact difference = ?

Unit 5 Review

Check Yourself

1. Suppose you are at a football game. Tell three amounts you might want to estimate.

2. For each problem, use round numbers to estimate the difference.

   a. 85 − 29 = ?

   b. 544 − 287 = ?

   c. 8,291 − 4,716 = ?

   d. 48,427 − 8,603 = ?

3. For each problem, write whether the answer is **close** or **not close** to the estimate. Give your reason.

   a. estimate = 90

       answer = 82

   b. estimate = 20

       answer = 46

   c. estimate = 700

       answer = 595

   d. estimate = 400

       answer = 612

   e. estimate = 9,500

       answer = 9,824

   f. estimate = 1,200

       answer = 1,117

4. In this problem, the answer is not close to the estimate. Tell what the mistake is. Then copy the problem and solve it correctly. Check your answer.

$$622 - 158 = ?$$

	622 ≈	600		622	
	158 ≈	− 200		− 158	
		400 estimate		664 answer	

5. Estimate, subtract, compare, and check to find the correct answer for each problem.

   a. 75 − 27 = ?

   b. 567 − 429 = ?

   c. 6,445 − 3,957 = ?

   d. 48,936 − 7,618 = ?

6. Suppose you must unpack 125 crates. You unpack 68 of them. Estimate to find *about* how many more crates you must unpack. Then find the exact number. Compare and check.

7. To complete each sentence below, write the correct word from this list:

   about   **estimate**   **exact**

   a. You _?_ to figure about what an amount is.

   b. An estimate can help you see if your _?_ answer makes sense.

   c. The sign ≈ means *is _?_ equal to.*

Bonus

Make a poster that shows how to estimate the difference between two numbers:
First, show how to estimate with numbers that fill the same places. Then show how to estimate with numbers that *don't* fill all the same places.

Real-Life Subtracting

Figuring Amounts in Real Life

In this book, you worked on improving your math skills. You learned ways to subtract correctly and make sure your answers are correct. You'll need to use those skills to figure amounts in real life. You'll also need to know *when* to use those skills.

For example, suppose:

- You must drive to another town. You want to figure which is the shortest route to that town.
- You must finish a job by a certain time. You want to know how many hours you have left to do it.
- You want to buy a house. You need to know how much more money you must have to make a down payment.

Do you subtract to find each amount? Or do you add, multiply, or divide? What numbers do you figure with?

In this unit, you'll solve real-life problems like the ones above. You'll learn how to decide what amounts to figure, what numbers to use, and when subtracting is the right math operation for solving a problem. You'll also use the math skills you've learned to estimate differences, figure exact differences, and check your answers.

As you work through this unit, you will see that what you've learned in math class can help you in real life—every day.

Exercise

Write two examples of when you subtracted outside math class in the past week. Tell what amounts you needed to figure and why you needed to know them.

Figuring a Difference

Suppose you are solving a word problem in class. You first read the problem, then you go through these steps:

Step a: You decide what amount you must find.

Step b: You decide what numbers to figure with.

Step c: You decide which math operation to use by thinking of why that operation would solve the problem.

Step d: You then write a number problem and work it out.

Now, suppose this happens when you are *out* of school:

> You are having a "yard sale." In your front yard, you put out things that you want to sell—chairs, dishes, books, clothes, and so on. A person wants to buy a chair that you are selling for $12. She gives you a $20 bill. How much will you give back to her?

That is an example of a subtraction problem that happens in real life. To solve it, you think through the same steps that you follow to solve word problems in math class:

To solve real-life math problems

a. Decide what amount to find.

b. Decide what numbers to figure with.

c. Decide what math operation to use and why.

d. Work out the problem.

a. Find how much to give back in change.

b. Figure with 20 (dollars) and 12 (dollars).

c. Subtract because you must find what is left from 20 when you take away 12.

d. Work out the problem like this:

20 dollars—amount given

−12 dollars—price for the chair

8 dollars change

Exercise

Follow the example in the lesson. For each problem:

    a. Tell what amount to find.

    b. Tell what numbers to figure with.

    c. Tell why you should *subtract*.

    d. Work the math problem.

1. You take $6 to the theater. You spend $3 for a ticket. You want to know how much money you have left for food.

2. You want to recycle 10 pounds of cans. You have 3 pounds. You want to know how many more pounds of cans you need.

3. Your team plays 8 games a year. You play 5 games. You want to know how many games are left to play.

4. At the store, you find one binder for $6. You find another binder for $4. You want to know how much you'll save if you buy the cheaper binder.

5. You are playing Scrabble with a friend. You score 18 points on your turn. Your friend scores 9 points. You want to know how many points ahead you are.

Figuring on Paper

In the last lesson you worked with problems that had two- or one-digit numbers. You probably could have worked those problems in your head.

In real life, you'll often have to subtract numbers with many digits. To make sure you figure correctly, you should work those problems on paper. You should also use what you learned to estimate the differences, work the problems, and check your answers.

Here is an example of a real-life problem that should be worked on paper:

> You are filling the gas tank of your car. You want to know how many miles your car will travel from one fill-up to the next. So you look at the *odometer* on the dashboard—the meter that counts each mile that the car travels. It shows a total of 68,497 miles. The next time you fill the tank, you look at the odometer again. It shows a new total: 68,612 miles.

a. Find how many miles the car goes from one fill-up to the next.

b. Figure with 68,612 (total miles) and 68,497 (total miles).

c. Subtract because you must find the difference between the total miles.

d. Work out the problem like this:

$$
\begin{array}{r}
68{,}612 \text{ last total miles} \\
- \ 68{,}497 \text{ first total miles} \\
\hline
115 \text{ miles difference}
\end{array}
$$

To solve real-life math problems:
a. Decide what amount to find.
b. Decide what numbers to figure with.
c. Decide what math operation to use and why.
d. Work out the problem.

Exercise

Follow the example in the lesson. For each problem:

a. Tell what amount to find.
b. Tell what numbers to figure with.
c. Tell why you should *subtract*.
d. Set up a number problem. Then solve it: estimate, subtract, compare, and check.

1. You read about two of the tallest mountains in the world. Mt. Everest is 29,028 feet tall and Mt. Kanchenjunga is 28,208 feet tall. You want to figure the difference in their heights.

2. You need to stamp 225 letters at work. You stamp 78 of them. You want to know how many more letters you need to stamp.

3. You want to buy a television set. You find a set you like for $368. You find another set you like for $515. You want to compare the prices.

4. Your pay for the month is $1,471. But $194 from that amount will be used for insurance and savings. You want to know how much of your pay you will have left.

5. In 1986, the California Angels won 92 baseball games. The Seattle Mariners won 67 games. You want to know how many more games the Angels won than the Mariners.

6. Your soccer league wants to raise $5,000. So far, you have raised $3,467. You need to report how much more money must be raised.

Deciding What Numbers to Use

When you figure differences, you'll sometimes have several numbers to work with. You'll have to decide *which* of those numbers to use. First ask yourself: What two *same things* am I finding the difference between? Then choose the numbers that stand for those same things and subtract.

For example, suppose you work in a restaurant. In the morning, you make 40 tuna salads and 40 taco salads. In the afternoon, 17 tuna salads and 8 taco salads are left.

How many taco salads were sold?

To figure the difference, use the numbers that stand for *taco* salads:

```
   40  taco salads
 −  8  taco salads
    ?  taco salads
```

How many tuna salads were sold?

To figure the difference, use the numbers that stand for tuna salads:

```
   40  tuna salads
 − 17  tuna salads
    ?  tuna salads
```

How many more taco salads than tuna salads are left?

You are now finding the difference between salads that are left, so, use the numbers that stand for them:

```
   17  tuna salads left
 −  8  taco salads left
    ?  more tuna salads
```

Copy the three math problems on notepaper and solve them. First, estimate each difference. Then, subtract to find the exact answer. Next, compare your estimate and answer. Check your answer. What are the differences?

SALE!
Wool Sweaters **$21**

Shop this Friday and
Saturday - take another
$5 off our sale price.

$2	**Coupon**	$2
	$2 off any purchase	
$2	(valid every day but Fri, Sat.)	$2

Exercise

For each problem:

a. Tell what amount to figure.

b. Tell what numbers to use.

c. Tell why you should *subtract*.

d. Work the math problem. (Be sure to compare and check.)

You read an ad for sweaters. The sweaters are on sale for $21 each. They cost $5 less on Friday or Saturday. They cost $2 less Sunday through Thursday if you use the ad coupon.

1. You want to buy a sweater on Saturday. You want to know how much money you will need.

2. You want to shop for a sweater on Sunday. You will take the ad coupon with you. How much money will you need for the sweater?

You see a car that you like at a car dealer's place. It costs $9,688. That price includes the costs of these extra features:

air conditioning — $535
radio/cassette player — $396
sunroof — $459

3. You want to figure the price for the car with everything except the air conditioning.

4. You want to know the price for everything but the sunroof.

5. You want to figure the car's price *without* the radio/cassette player.

Estimating Differences

Imagine this:

You need to buy a set of tires. You can buy one set for $68. Or, you can spend $92 for a better set. You wonder *about how much more* you'd spend if you buy the better set.

That is an example of a time you might *only estimate* a difference. You don't need to know the exact difference between the tire prices. So, you can just round the prices and estimate the difference:

$$\begin{array}{r} \$92 \approx \$90 \\ \$68 \approx -\ \$70 \\ \hline \$20 \quad \text{difference} \end{array}$$

Your estimate shows you would spend about $20 more for the better tires. Now you can decide whether they are worth it.

Exercise

For each problem:
a. Tell what difference you need to estimate.
b. Tell what numbers to use.
c. Round the numbers.
d. Estimate the difference.

1. You need to read a 258-page book for class. So far, you have read 121 pages. You want to know about how many more pages you have to read.

2. Your class ends at 43 minutes past the hour. It's now 24 minutes past the hour. You want to know about how many more minutes you have before class ends.

3. Your team has $238. You plan to spend $192 for team shirts. You want to figure about how much money you'll have left if you buy them.

4. You're driving to a town 281 miles away. The tripometer in your car shows you have gone 137 miles since you started. You want to figure about how many more miles you have to go.

Subtracting in a Check Register

Suppose you have a checking account. You take out money from it by writing checks. To keep track of the money you take out and the money you have left, you use the *check register* in your checkbook. That is a form on which you write information about your checks and your *balance*—how much is left in your account after you subtract each check.

Most check registers look something like the one shown on this page. In this example, information about each check is written on an uncolored row. Each new balance is written on a colored row.

CHECK NUMBER	DATE	DESCRIPTION	AMOUNT		
			$235	**starting balance**	2 3 5
101	1/23	school fees	22	**amount of check**	− 2 2
			213	**new balance**	2 1 3
102	1/25	U-Save (food)	18		− 1 8
					?
103	1/26	Shop Mart (pants)	36		− 3 6
					?
104	1/30	Cash	25		− 2 5
					?

Find the *starting balance*. That is the amount of money that was put into the account. Now look at the information about the first check. That check is for $22. So, $22 should be subtracted. What is the new balance after that amount is subtracted?

Exercise

Continue finding each new balance by subtracting amounts for these checks:

1. check 102   **2.** check 103   **3.** check 104

Knowing When to Subtract

You worked on building up your subtracting skills in this book. So, all the problems you worked on were subtraction problems. In real life, of course, all problems are *not* subtraction problems. You will sometimes have to use another math operation to solve a problem: you may need to add, multiply, or divide.

How can you tell when you should subtract to solve a problem? All subtraction problems have certain things about them that are the same. The chart on this page lists those things. They are *clues* that tell you to subtract. Look them over. Then find the clues in the examples at right.

Clues to Subtracting	Examples
SUBTRACT when: 1. You need to find: • **how much more or less** one number is than another. • **how much is left** from a number when you take away an amount. • **how much more you need** to make a number larger. 2. You figure with only two numbers. 3. The numbers stand for the same kind of things.	Karim is 6 feet tall. Abdul is 5 feet tall. What is the difference in their heights? 6 feet − 5 feet = 1 foot You must drive 115 miles. So far, you've driven 23 miles. How many miles are left to drive? 115 miles − 23 miles = 92 miles left You want to buy a coat that costs $25. You have $16. How much more do you need? $25 − $16 = $9 more needed

Exercise

For each problem:

a. Tell what amount to find.

b. Tell what numbers to figure with.

c. Write **subtract** or **don't subtract**.

d. If you write *subtract,* then work the problem. If you write *don't subtract,* then tell why not. (One is done as an example.)

1. You deliver 23 packages before lunch. You deliver 39 packages after lunch. You need to report how many packages you deliver in all.

> 1.
> a. Find the total packages.
> b. The numbers to figure with are 23 packages and 39 packages.
> c. Don't subtract.
> d. The answer is not a difference.

2. You can make $4 an hour working at a grocery store. You can make $6 working at a gas station. You want to know how much more you would make at the gas station.

3. There should be 1,450 books in the library. There are only 827. You need to report how many library books are missing.

4. You want to buy 5 pounds of bananas. Each pound of bananas costs 19¢. You want to know how much you'll need to pay.

5. Your band has 4 members. The band earns $375 by playing at a party. You need to give each band member the same amount of money.

6. You must make 48 payments to pay back a loan. So far, you have made 29 payments. You want to know how many more payments you must make.

7. Your friend weighs 109 pounds. A month ago, she weighed 122 pounds. You want to figure how many pounds she lost.

8. You make $564 each month working at a day care center. You want to figure how much money you'll make in 9 months.

Unit 6 Review

Check Yourself

1. Suppose you go to the store with $50 to buy a jacket. You find one jacket for $42. You find another jacket for $36.

   a. Tell two amounts you might want to figure by subtracting.

   b. Tell what numbers you would use to figure each amount.

2. Read each problem. If it is a subtraction problem, set up a number problem for it and solve it. If it is *not* a subtraction problem, write **don't subtract** and tell why you say so.

   a. You need to win 325 tickets for the arcade prize you want. So far, you have 267 tickets. You want to know how many more tickets you need.

   b. You need $8 for a binder. You need $15 for a textbook. You want to know how much money you need for both things.

3. For each problem below, tell what amount to figure. Then work the number problem—estimate, subtract, compare, and check.

   a. You are reading about skyscrapers. You read that the CN Tower in Toronto is 1,821 feet tall. And the Sears Tower in Chicago is 1,454 feet tall. You wonder what the difference in heights is.

   b. There are 184 days in the school year. You have gone to school for 25 days so far. You want to know how many days of school are left.

4. Think up two examples of these real-life math problems. Write each example first as a word problem. Then write it as a number problem and solve it.

   a. A subtraction problem about shopping.

   b. A subtraction problem about traveling.

   c. A subtraction problem about work.

5. Copy each sentence and finish it. Use the correct word from this list.

difference	**less**	**same**
different	**only**	

   a. You subtract to find the __?__ between amounts.

   b. You figure with __?__ two numbers.

   c. The numbers stand for the __?__ kind of things.

Bonus

Choose something you'd like to buy (such as a stereo). Go to three stores that sell that item. Find one you like in each store.

On paper, describe each one you choose and list its price. Then subtract to compare prices. Decide which one you'd buy and tell why.

Subtraction Review

Check Yourself

1. The steps below tell how to solve this problem. But they are out of order. Copy the problem. Then write the steps in the correct order.

$$
\begin{array}{r} 402 \\ -\ 139 \\ \hline \end{array}
$$

   a. Regroup a ten as ones.
   b. Subtract tens.
   c. Subtract ones.
   d. Estimate.
   e. Regroup a hundred as tens.
   f. Compare and check.
   g. Subtract hundreds.

2. Set up each problem. Subtract. Be sure to estimate, compare, and check.

   a. $593 - 442 = ?$
   b. $5{,}857 - 2{,}846 = ?$
   c. $3{,}654 - 3{,}247 = ?$
   d. $648 - 589 = ?$
   e. $507 - 468 = ?$
   f. $9{,}005 - 6{,}346 = ?$
   g. $70{,}002 - 4{,}265 = ?$
   h. $5{,}837 - 9 = ?$

3. Suppose you run a business. One day you take in $432 altogether. $346 is from snack bar sales. The rest is from souvenir sales. During the day, you also pay out $117 altogether. $65 is for supplies and the rest is for other bills.

   a. How much did you take in for souvenir sales?
   b. How much more did you make in snack bar sales than in souvenir sales?
   c. How much did you pay for other bills?
   d. How much did you have left at the end of the day?

4. Read the graph. Then use it to answer the questions below it.

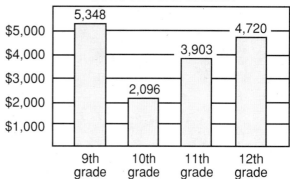

SCHOOL FUND RAISER

   a. How much more did the 9th grade raise than the 10th grade?
   b. How much more did the 12th grade raise than the 11th grade?

5. Read each problem. If it is a subtraction problem, set up a number problem for it and solve it. If it is *not* a subtraction problem, write **don't subtract** and tell why you say so.

   a. You pick 56 pounds of tomatoes. You sell 25 pounds of them at a farmers' market. You want to know how many pounds you have left.
   b. You pick 56 pounds of tomatoes. You plan to pack them in 5-pound bags. You want to know how many bags you'll need.

Bonus

Go to a bank. Find out when a *bank teller* needs to subtract on the job. Find out what happens if a teller subtracts wrong. Tell your class what you learn.

A Glossary of Math Words

These words are used to describe the basic operations of addition, subtraction, multiplication, and division.

an swer bar   The line in a problem between the numbers that are figured and the answer.

av er age   The answer to a certain kind of division problem; the number you get when you divide a sum by the number of its parts.

col umn   A line of digits that are one on top of another; a row of digits that go up or down.

dif fer ence   The answer to a subtraction problem.

dig it   A symbol used to make numbers. There are ten digits: 1, 2, 3, 4, 5, 6, 7, 8, 9, 0.

div i dend   The number that is divided.

di vi sor   The number that divides another number; the number that another number is divided by.

es ti mate   To figure *about* what an amount is.

ex act num bers   The actual numbers of a problem.

line up   To write digits that have the same place value in a straight column.

op po site   Completely different. For example: *plus* is the opposite of *minus*.

place   The position of a digit in a number. For example: in the number 12, the digit 2 is in one place and the digit 1 is in another.

place val ue   The kind of amount each place stands for. For example: in the number 12, the digit 2 has a place value of *ones*; the digit 1 has a place value of *tens*.

prod uct   The answer to a multiplication problem.

quo tient   The answer to a division problem.

re group   To change an amount in one form to another form that has an equal value. For example, 12 can be regrouped as 1 ten and 2 ones.

re main der   The number left over when a number cannot be divided evenly.

round   To change a number to the closest number that ends in 0.

set up   To write a problem by lining up its numbers correctly.

sum   The answer to an addition problem.

sym bol   A mark that stands for an idea. For example, + stands for *add*.

Tables of Basic Facts

To Add or Multiply

1. Find one of the (dark) numbers at the left of the chart. Go *across* its row.

2. Find the other (dark) number at the top of the chart. Go *down* its row.

3. The answer is the light number in the square where the two rows meet.

Addition: Add dark left numbers and dark top numbers.

	1	2	3	4	5	6	7	8	9
1	2	3	4	5	6	7	8	9	10
2	3	4	5	6	7	8	9	10	11
3	4	5	6	7	8	9	10	11	12
4	5	6	7	8	9	10	11	12	13
5	6	7	8	9	10	11	12	13	14
6	7	8	9	10	11	12	13	14	15
7	8	9	10	11	12	13	14	15	16
8	9	10	11	12	13	14	15	16	17
9	10	11	12	13	14	15	16	17	18

Multiplication: Multiply dark left numbers by dark top numbers.

	1	2	3	4	5	6	7	8	9
1	1	2	3	4	5	6	7	8	9
2	2	4	6	8	10	12	14	16	18
3	3	6	9	12	15	18	21	24	27
4	4	8	12	16	20	24	28	32	36
5	5	10	15	20	25	30	35	40	45
6	6	12	18	24	30	36	42	48	54
7	7	14	21	28	35	42	49	56	63
8	8	16	24	32	40	48	56	64	72
9	9	18	27	36	45	54	63	72	81

To Subtract or Divide

1. Find one of the (dark) numbers at the left of the chart. Go *across* its row until you find the other (light) number.

2. Go up the row that the other (light) number is in.

3. The answer is the dark top number.

Subtraction: Subtract dark left numbers from light numbers.

	1	2	3	4	5	6	7	8	9
1	2	3	4	5	6	7	8	9	10
2	3	4	5	6	7	8	9	10	11
3	4	5	6	7	8	9	10	11	12
4	5	6	7	8	9	10	11	12	13
5	6	7	8	9	10	11	12	13	14
6	7	8	9	10	11	12	13	14	15
7	8	9	10	11	12	13	14	15	16
8	9	10	11	12	13	14	15	16	17
9	10	11	12	13	14	15	16	17	18

Division: Divide dark left numbers into light numbers.

	1	2	3	4	5	6	7	8	9
1	1	2	3	4	5	6	7	8	9
2	2	4	6	8	10	12	14	16	18
3	3	6	9	12	15	18	21	24	27
4	4	8	12	16	20	24	28	32	36
5	5	10	15	20	25	30	35	40	45
6	6	12	18	24	30	36	42	48	54
7	7	14	21	28	35	42	49	56	63
8	8	16	24	32	40	48	56	64	72
9	9	18	27	36	45	54	63	72	81